Experiments
with
ELECTRICITY

Isabel Thomas

heinemann
raintree

Edited by Clare Lewis and Amanda Robbins
Designed by Steve Mead
Picture research by Eric Gohl
Production by Victoria Fitzgerald
Originated by Capstone Global Library Ltd
Printed and bound by CTPS in China

19 18 17 16 15 14
10 9 8 7 6 5 4 3 2 1

Library of Congress Cataloging-in-Publication Data
Thomas, Isabel, 1979- author.
  Experiments with electricity / Isabel Thomas.
    pages cm.—(Read and experiment)
  Summary: "Explore the world of electricity with engaging
text, real life examples and fun step-by-step experiments. This
book brings the science of electricity to life, explaining the
concepts then getting kids to be hands-on scientists!"—Pro-
vided by publisher.
  Includes bibliographical references and index.
  ISBN 978-1-4109-6838-8 (hb)—ISBN 978-1-4109-7902-5 (pb)
ISBN 978-1-4109-6843-2 (ebooks) 1. Electricity—Experiments—Juvenile literature. 2. Electricity—Juvenile literature.
I. Title.

QC527.2.T46 2015
537.078—dc23   2014016120

This book has been officially leveled by using the F&P Text
Level Gradient™ Leveling System.

Acknowledgments
We would like to thank the following for permission to
reproduce photographs: Dreamstime: Didlatof, 6 (top middle);
Glow Images: Science Photo Library/Richard Bailey, 4;
Shutterstock: Andrey_Kuzmin, 22 (bottom right), baloon111,
23, Feliks Gurevich, 6 (bottom), Kreatif Multimedia, 22
(bottom left), Kuzma, 22 (bottom middle), Steve Cukrov, 22
(top middle), Studio BM, 6 (top left), Sumit Buranarothtrakul,
6 (top right), Yuganov Konstantin, 22 (top right)

All other photographs were created at Capstone Studio by
Karon Dubke.

We would like to thank Patrick O'Mahony for his invaluable
help in the preparation of this book.

Every effort has been made to contact copyright holders of
material reproduced in this book. Any omissions will be
rectified in subsequent printings if notice is given to the
publisher.

All the Internet addresses (URLs) given in this book were valid
at the time of going to press. However, due to the dynamic
nature of the Internet, some addresses may have changed, or
sites may have changed or ceased to exist since publication.
While the author and publisher regret any inconvenience this
may cause readers, no responsibility for any such changes can
be accepted by either the author or the publisher.

ADULT HELP

Safety instructions for adult helper
The experiments in this book should be planned and carried out with adult supervision. Certain steps should
only be carried out by an adult—these are indicated in the text. Always follow the instructions carefully, and
take extra care when using scissors (pg. 18), flashlight bulbs (pg. 12), and batteries (pg. 12 and pg. 24). Avoid
short-circuiting batteries—more information is given below. *Never* experiment or play with the electricity in
your home or poke anything into a wall outlet. Remember that burst balloons can be a choking hazard. The
publisher and author disclaim, to the maximum extent possible, all liability for any accidents, injuries or losses
that may occur as a result of the information or instructions in this book.

Information about batteries
The experiments in this book are designed for use with AA batteries. A 3v Lithium coin battery is used in
experiment 3 (pg. 18). Do not use batteries with a higher voltage.

Wires used to build circuits should be around 10 inches long. Never connect the negative terminal of a
battery directly to the positive terminal. This could short circuit the battery, which is dangerous. Do not use
rechargeable batteries, which can draw a high current if short-circuited. Never insert fingers, wires or any
objects into a wall socket.

Contents

Some words are shown in bold, **like this**. You can find out what they mean by looking in the glossary.

Why Experiment?

How does a flashlight work? Why does a balloon cling to walls when you rub it on a sweater? Can a lemon make a noise?

You can answer all these questions by investigating **electricity**!

Scientists ask questions like these. They find the answers with the help of **experiments**.

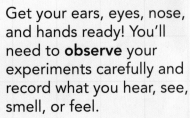

Get your ears, eyes, nose, and hands ready! You'll need to **observe** your experiments carefully and record what you hear, see, smell, or feel.

An experiment is a test that has been carefully planned to help answer a question. The experiments in this book will help you to understand how electricity works. You'll learn how to work like a scientist, and have lots of fun along the way!

 ## IS IT A FAIR TEST?

Most experiments involve changing something to see what happens. Make sure you only change one thing, or **variable**, at a time. Then you will know that it was the variable you changed that made the difference. This is called a fair test.

WARNING! Electricity can be very dangerous. Ask an adult to help you plan and carry out each experiment. Follow the instructions carefully. Look out for this sign.

ADULT HELP

Follow these steps to work like a scientist:

Ask a question.

Come up with an idea to test.

Plan an experiment.

What will you change?
What will you keep the same?
What will you measure?

Make a **prediction**.

Observe carefully.

Work out what the results mean.

Answer the question!

What Is Electricity?

What do this robot, car, and excavator have in common, apart from being fun to use?

They are all powered by electricity. **Electricity** is a form of **energy**. It can be changed into other types of energy easily. This makes it very useful.

In an iron, electricity is changed into heat energy. In a light bulb, it is changed into light energy. In a doorbell, it is changed into sound energy. In a washing machine, it is changed into movement energy.

REAL WORLD SCIENCE

LEDs are small lights that glow when electricity flows through them. LEDs are tough and bright. Can you spot them in traffic lights?

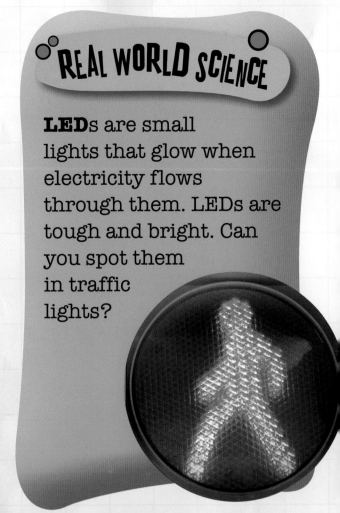

From place to place

Electricity flows through metal wires a bit like water flows through a pipe. This makes electricity a useful way to transfer energy from place to place.

Most of the electricity we use comes from power stations. Anything that plugs into a wall outlet uses electricity. We also get electricity from batteries. A battery uses chemicals to produce electricity.

WARNING!
Mains electricity is much more powerful than the electricity provided by batteries. Never experiment with mains electricity.

Can a lemon be a battery? Find out on page 8.

REAL WORLD SCIENCE

Our homes and schools are full of **devices** that use electricity. How many can you spot? Use a Venn diagram to show if they use electricity, batteries, or both. Hint: Do you have to plug them into an outlet, or are they portable?

Make Your Own Battery

Some fruits and vegetables can be turned into batteries. Experiment to find out which ones make the best batteries.

Equipment

- Different fruits and vegetables, such as potato, lemon, kiwi, grapefruit, apple
- Pennies
- Paper clips
- Thin **insulated wire**
- Plastic tape
- Buzzer

Tip: Roll the lemon on a table first, to squish the insides.

Method

1 Ask an adult to make two cuts in a lemon. Push a copper coin into one cut, and a paper clip into the other. Make sure the penny and paper clip don't touch.

2 Ask an adult to strip the insulation from the ends of the wire.

ADULT HELP

3 Touch the coin and paper clip with the wires attached to your buzzer. Does the buzzer make a sound?

4 Try adding another lemon. Push a copper coin and paper clip into the second lemon. Use wire to join the paper clip in the first lemon to the coin in the second lemon.

5 Touch the wires from your buzzer to the coin of the first lemon and the paperclip of the second lemon. Does the buzzer sound?

6 Try using different fruits and vegetables. Which makes the loudest buzz?

Conclusion

A battery uses chemicals to make electricity. Most batteries contain two different metals separated by a third substance. By pushing two different metals into a lemon, you can make a simple battery. The lemon juice is the third substance. When you connect the battery to a buzzer, **chemical changes** happen that make electricity flow.

Never eat or cook with fruit and vegetables that have been used to make batteries.

What Is a Circuit?

Electricity can only flow around a complete path, called a **circuit**. If the path is broken, no electricity will flow.

We can't usually tell if electricity is flowing through a wire, but we can tell if electricity is flowing through a light bulb, buzzer, or motor. Bulbs, buzzers, and motors are called **components**. When you add components to a circuit, the electricity flows through them as well.

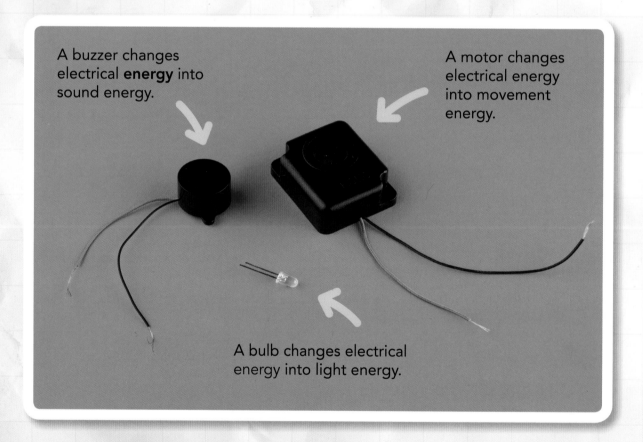

A buzzer changes electrical **energy** into sound energy.

A motor changes electrical energy into movement energy.

A bulb changes electrical energy into light energy.

Can you find any toys or household objects that use bulbs, buzzers, or motors?

Build this circuit using a battery, two wires, and an **LED**. When the circuit is complete, electricity will flow around it, and the LED will glow. Try breaking the circuit. Does the LED glow? Try turning the battery around. Does the LED glow?

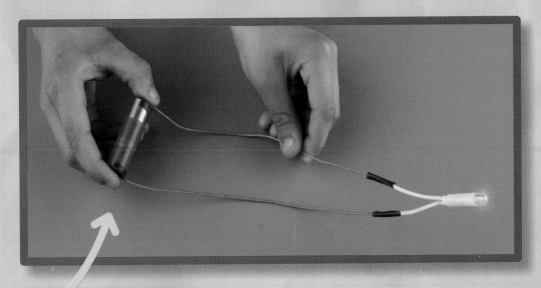

Remember that electricity will only flow if there is a complete loop from one end of the battery back to the other end of the battery.

REAL WORLD SCIENCE

A battery has a positive (+) and a negative (-) end. In your lemon battery (see page 8), the penny was the positive end and the paperclip was the negative end.

Design a Flashlight

Take a flashlight apart, and you'll find a simple **circuit** made up of:

- one or more batteries
- a loop of material that **electricity** can travel through
- one or more flashlight bulbs.

Experiment with circuit making to design your own torch.

Equipment

- Three 1.5 v torch bulbs in bulb holders
- Three AA batteries
- Plastic tape
- Thin **insulated wire**, with the insulation stripped off at the ends (see page 8)

1 Make a circuit using one battery and one bulb. Does the bulb light up when the circuit is complete? Record what you see.

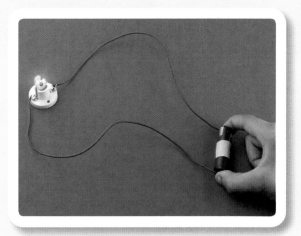

2 Add another bulb to the circuit. Do both bulbs light up when the circuit is complete? How bright are they? Can you light three bulbs with one battery?

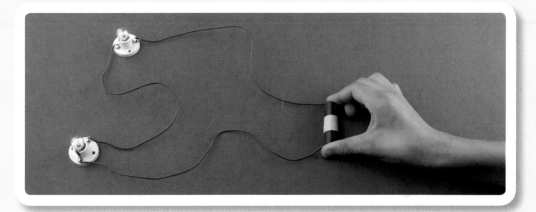

3 Now test two batteries with one bulb, then two batteries with two bulbs. Record what you see. Does adding more batteries make the bulbs brighter or dimmer?

Make sure both batteries are the same way around.

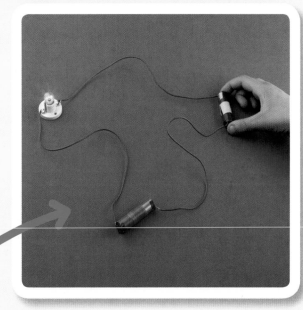

Number of Batteries	Number of Bulbs	What I see
1	1	
1	2	
1	3	
2	1	
2	2	
2	3	
3	3	
3	2	
3	1	

Draw a table like this to record what you see (your **observations**). Do the bulbs light up? Are they bright or dim?

4 How many batteries do you need to add to the **circuit** to light three bulbs brightly? What happens if you use three batteries and one bulb?

IS IT A FAIR TEST?

Make sure you only change one thing at a time—the number of batteries or the number of bulbs. Is the total length of wire the same in every circuit? How could you make your **experiment** fairer?

Use your results to design a flashlight that is bright, but not too heavy to carry around.

Conclusion

Components have to share the electrical **energy** that flows around a circuit. When you add more bulbs without adding more batteries, the bulbs get dimmer. When you add more batteries, more electrical energy flows around the circuit. This makes bulbs brighter. If you add too many batteries, the bulbs may burn out.

What Can Electricity Flow Through?

Some materials let **electricity** flow through them. We call these materials **conductors**. Copper wires are good conductors. They let electricity travel through them so the bulb lights up.

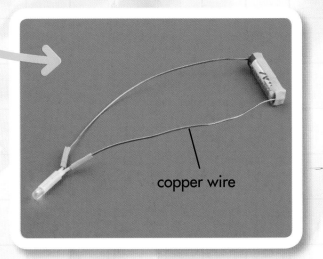

copper wire

Other materials do not allow electricity to flow through them. They are called **insulators**. These copper wires have a plastic coating. Plastic is an insulator. Electricity cannot travel through the plastic, so the bulb does not light up.

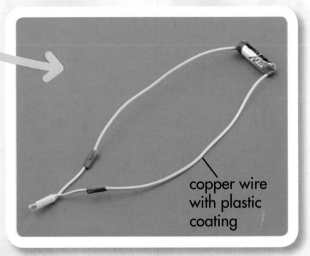

copper wire with plastic coating

Water is a good conductor. There is lots of water in our bodies, so electricity can flow through people. This makes electricity very dangerous. It can damage our bodies if it flows through us.

Copper wires are used to carry electricity inside electrical cables. Why do you think the cables have a plastic coating?

SEE THE SCIENCE ⇣

Rub a balloon against a wool sweater and hold it over some torn-up tissue paper.

The paper clings to the balloon, showing that "static" electricity has built up on the balloon. This is electricity that stays in one place. It cannot flow away because rubber is an insulator. Try rubbing a metal spoon on the wool sweater. Does it attract the tissue paper?

Make a Robot

Amaze your friends by making a robot that can identify **conductors** and **insulators**!

Equipment

- Small cardboard box
- Aluminum foil
- Scissors
- Pencil
- Sticky tape
- 3V Lithium coin battery
- **LED**
- Three pieces of **insulated wire**, with the ends stripped (see page 8)
- Household objects made of different materials, such as metal, plastic, wood, glass, ceramics, fabrics, and rubber

ADULT HELP

Method

1 Decorate the box to look like a robot. Make a small hole in the top of the box, and one on each side.

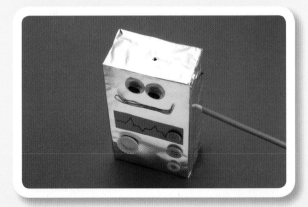

2 Tape a piece of insulated wire to each end of the battery. Join the insulated wire from the positive (+) end of the battery to the long LED wire. Use tape to hold it in place.

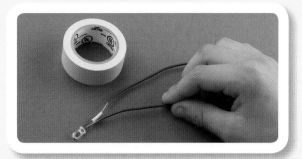

Tip: Make sure all the connections are fastened tightly. If there is a gap in the **circuit**, the **electricity** will not flow.

3 Attach the third insulated wire to the short LED wire.

4 Push the LED up through the small hole in your robot's head. Carefully tape it in place.

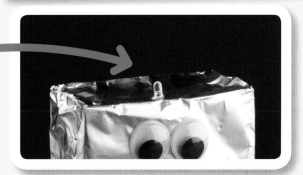

5 Feed the ends of the wires through the holes at the side of the box to create your robot's arms. Tape the battery to the inside of the box.

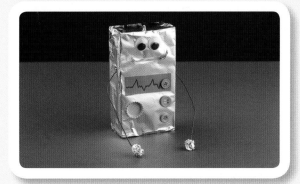

6 Wrap the end of each arm in foil to make your robot's hands. When the robot's arms are apart, the circuit is broken and electricity does not flow. Test your robot by putting his hands together. Does the LED glow?

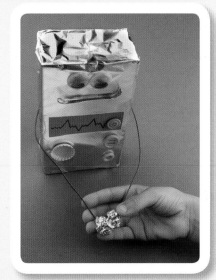

Tip: If the LED does not glow, check that all the **components** are connected properly. Try connecting the LED the other way around.

7 Now put your robot to work! Your robot can find out if materials conduct **electricity** by touching them with both hands.

When the robot's arms both touch a **conductor**, it completes the **circuit**. Electricity flows around the circuit, through the conductor, and makes the **LED** glow.

When the robot's arms both touch an **insulator**, the circuit is broken because electricity cannot flow through the insulator. The LED does not glow.

 IS IT A FAIR TEST?

Make this a fair test by testing materials of the same length or size. How else could you improve your **experiment**?

8 Copy and complete this table to record which materials make the LED glow.

Material tested	Does the LED glow?
Metal spoon	Yes
Plastic ruler	No
Rubber	

9 **Analyze** your results. Which materials are conductors? Which are insulators?

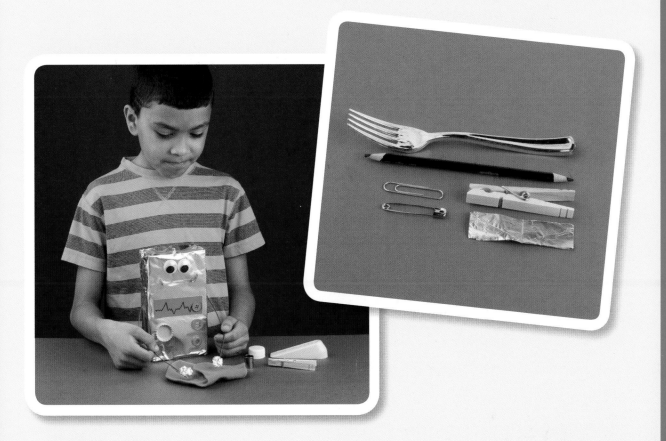

Conclusion

Electricity can only flow around a circuit if every part of the circuit is a conductor. Most metals are good conductors.

Materials such as plastic, glass, wood, rubber, ceramics, and cardboard are insulators. They do not allow electricity to flow through them.

Do not insert the robot's arms or any other objects into a wall outlet.

Breaking Circuits

Nobody wants their flashlight, toaster, or toy robot to stay on all the time. A **switch** is a way of controlling a **circuit**, so **electricity** flows when we want it to.

Electricity will only flow around a circuit with no gaps (a **complete circuit**). When you press a switch, you make or break a circuit.

SEE THE SCIENCE ⬇

How many different types of switches can you find in your home or school?

Switches are a handy and safe way to let electricity flow around a circuit, or stop it from flowing.

Turning a switch off makes a gap in the circuit. Electricity stops flowing.

Turning a switch on closes the gap. The circuit is complete and electricity starts flowing.

REAL WORLD SCIENCE

Electricity can be very dangerous. A shock from an electrical outlet can kill. Many homes have special switches that turn themselves off if there is a problem. This breaks the circuit very quickly, so electricity stops flowing.

Remember that water conducts electricity. You should never touch plugs, outlets, or switches with wet hands. Electricity could flow through the water to your body and give you an electric shock.

Switch It!

A **switch** can let **electricity** flow around a **circuit** or stop it from flowing. Can you make different switches to do different jobs?

Equipment

- Battery
- **Insulated wire** with ends stripped
- Buzzer and / or **LED**
- Thick cardboard
- Paperclips
- Pins
- Paper fasteners
- Small piece of plastic
- Aluminum foil
- Plastic tape

Ask an adult to strip the ends of the wires for you.

Method

Start by making a simple circuit with a buzzer. Test the circuit to make sure it works, but do not attach the second wire to the battery. Now make different switches to control the buzzer.

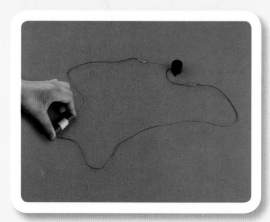

Switch 1

1 Cut a small rectangle of card. Push a paper fastener through each end. Fold the cardboard so the paper fasteners touch.

2 Turn the cardboard over. Connect the end of the wire attached to the buzzer to one paper fastener.

3 Use a third length of wire to join the other paper fastener to the battery.

4 Test the switch.

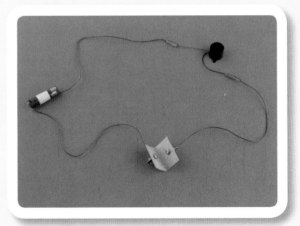

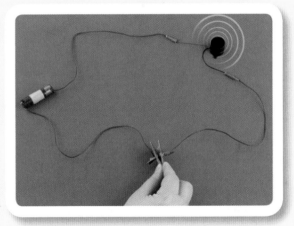

When the switch is open, there is a gap in the circuit. Electricity cannot flow across the gap, so the buzzer does not sound.

When you close the switch, you make the circuit complete. Electricity can flow around the circuit so the buzzer sounds.

Switch 2

1 Press two pins into a piece of plastic.

2 Wrap the end of the wire attached to the buzzer around one pin.

3 Use a third length of wire to join the other pin to the battery.

4 Loop a paperclip over one of the pins. Make sure it can touch the other pin when it moves. This is your **switch**.

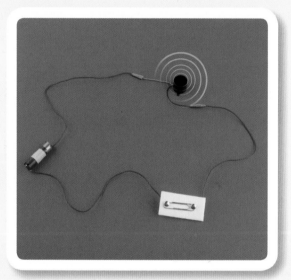 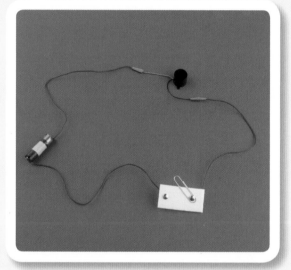

Switch 3

1 Cut two strips of cardboard. Wrap the end of each strip in foil.

2 Use tape to join the end of the wire attached to the buzzer to one of the foil ends.

3 Use a third length of wire to join the other piece of foil to the battery.

4 Arrange the pieces of cardboard so that one slides along the other. The switch is "on" when the foil ends touch.
What do you have to do to turn each switch on? Which switch is easiest to use? Can you design more switches?

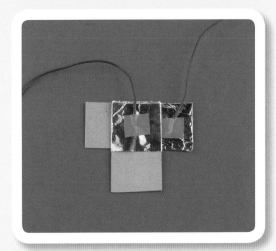

SEE THE SCIENCE ⬇

Which switch would be best for these circuits?

- A doorbell that sounds when someone steps on a doormat?

- A reading light?

- An alarm that sounds when you open a lid or door?

Can you make these devices using your buzzer and LED?

Conclusion

Switches let us control the flow of electricity around a circuit. When a switch is "off," there is a gap in the circuit. Electricity can't flow. When a switch is "on," the gap is closed. The circuit is complete, and electricity can flow.

Different switches work in different ways. To design a switch, you need a way to open a gap in the circuit when you want electricity to stop flowing, and close the gap when you want electricity to start flowing.

Plan Your Next Experiment!

Experiments have helped you discover some amazing things about electricity. Just like you, scientists carry out experiments to answer questions and test ideas. Each experiment is planned carefully to make it a fair test.

YOU ASKED...

YOU FOUND OUT THAT...

Can I use fruit or vegetables to make a battery?

- Electric currents transfer energy from place to place.
- A lemon can be turned into a battery, and used to make a buzzer sound.

What happens if you change the number of batteries or bulbs in a circuit?

- Adding more bulbs to a circuit make the bulbs dimmer.
- Adding more batteries makes the bulbs brighter.
- Bulbs and other components have to share the electricity that flows around a circuit.

Which materials can electricity flow through?

- Materials that let electricity flow through them are called conductors. Most metals are good conductors.
- Insulators do not let electricity pass through them.
- Electricity only flows around a circuit if every part of the circuit is made of a conductor.

How can I control the flow of electricity through a circuit?

- Electricity only keeps flowing around a complete (unbroken) circuit.
- A switch is a gap in a circuit that is easy to open and close.
- We use switches to control circuits, so electricity only flows when we want it to.
- Different types of switches are used for different jobs.

Experiments can also lead to new questions! Did you think of more questions about electricity? Can you plan new experiments to help answer them?

Remember that electricity from your home's outlets is very dangerous. Never experiment with this electricity. Use electrical devices. Keep water away from electricity.

WHAT NEXT?

→ How many fruit or vegetable 'batteries' would you need to make an LED glow? Plan an experiment to find out.

→ Do any non-metals conduct electricity? Plan an experiment to test different liquids (e.g. tap water, salt water, and soapy water), or the material at the center of different pencils.

→ What happens if you make a circuit with two switches? Do they both have to be closed for electricity to flow? Can you design and build a game using switches that make and break a circuit?

→ What happens if you change the length of a wire in a circuit? Plan an experiment to find out.

Glossary

analyze examine the results of an experiment carefully, in order to explain what happened

chemical a substance with particular properties

circuit path through which electricity flows

complete circuit electrical circuit with no gaps

component bulb, buzzer, motor or other device added to an electrical circuit

conductor material that allows electricity to flow through it

device piece of equipment made to do a certain job

electricity type of energy that flows from place to place through certain materials

energy power that makes something happen

experiment procedure carried out to test an idea or answer a question

insulated wire wire covered in an insulator

insulator material that does not allow electricity to flow through it

LED small light that glows when electricity flows through it

observe to note or measure what you see, hear, smell, or feel

prediction best guess or estimate of what will happen, based on what you already know

switch gap in a circuit that can be opened and closed easily

variable something that can be changed

Find Out More

Books

O'Donnell, Lian. *The Shocking World of Electricity*. (Graphic Science). Chicago: Heinemann Library, 2010

Oxlade, Chris. *It's Electric!* (Using Electricity). Chicago: Heinemann Library, 2013

Spilsbury, Louise and Richard. *Electricity*. Chicago, Heinemann Library, 2013

Web sites

FactHound offers a safe, fun way to find internet sites related to this book. All of the sites on FactHound have been researched by our staff.

Here's all you do:
Visit www.facthound.com
Type in this code: 9781410968388

Index

MAY 2 6 2015